Four Hands

Green

FOUR

Gulch

HANDS

Poems

DIANA SALTOON

ROBERT BRIGGS ASSOCIATES
San Francisco

Published by
Robert Briggs Associates
Box 9
Mill Valley, California 94942

Designed by Mark Ong
First Edition 1987

ISBN 0-931191-08-4

for Hillary

Outside the zendo
a low fog hides
the eucalyptus trees.
Within, facing dim white walls
black-robed souls
wander off misted trails.
Here and there,
rays lift the haze.

How tranquil
listening to steady breath
like the rhythm of female rain
when spring comes
to loosen hardened earth
and the harried mind
turns towards emptiness.

Hour after hour
keeping a straight back
on the black cushion,
a throbbing tension
opens more of me.

Between in and out breath
the brain pauses
and I rest
to listen
as other breath rises.

Beyond the window
all is soundless.

Hearing the ringing bell
wakens me to a moment when
seeing and feeling
sensations sharpen
a voice no longer
lost in the wind.

I laugh
because of fear
my hands clasp my tight belly
like a lid upon doubt
I dare not uncover.

How we suffer
and struggle against suffering
denouncing desire
and erecting removal that
like disappointing castles of sand
tempts and invites every tide.

The way I explain
the self to the self
is a risk.

Suffering roots of language
between mouth and ear
this back and forth within the mind
subverts understanding
and the silence of the One.

In the teahouse
the tokonoma
with simple flower and scroll
wakens ancient pleasure.
The kettle's hiss
warms the air
as mild summer wind
crosses the skin.

Whisked by my host
the cup of tea
heals and strengthens.

When the night's
no longer dark
but trembling with radiance
I stay with the moon
and enter curious dreams
of wider mystery.

Charged with silver'd grace
a keener eye
watches the dawn
transform another night.

Once more I've chased the friend
with too much clatter
clouding the air with thoughts
that little matter.

Turning to silence again
I long to still
mysterious intoxication.

In sweet silence
I enter a cathedral
within the body.

From a point
of new breath
I perceive
a light beyond day
a love beyond measure.

A dark ship slips
into a waiting ocean
upsetting the circling gulls
and disturbing a lone observer
on the beach below who,
peering into a dimm'd sky
is still concerned with knowing why.

Even at this hour
naked footprints mark the shore
of the revolving surf where
my own sink and match
those of many who came and went.

Pausing beneath shafts of sun
I watch a lone gull
above varied traces
that angry waves could not erase.

At night I hear
an insistent ocean
like some restless giant
rushing on the rocks
with disappearing fists
crashing carelessly
on forgiving sands.

Long visited by autumn
leaves cushion the trail
with pine, bay and eucalyptus
while random rays
spot copper and silver coins
in a meandering bed of water.

Who tossed coins
into this quiet harmony
who threw tokens of dream
into the melodious stream?
Or hoped some presence
in the scented air
would solve a recent problem
or ease an ancient pain?

Swimming in repeating sea
and innocent of a final wave
I sink into an endless night
to find and enter another light.

October cold
penetrates the zendo
adding discomfort to hours
of vain sitting
where I no longer
gather strength from breath
or the still shadow of Manjusri
who witnesses my distance.

Believing peace
we open other views
of here and there
of this and that
and you and I.

So when we meet
to seek more sun
let's see a way
near some middle place
to end this senseless strife.

The garden blooms
and the once-heard owl
from the eucalyptus
is gone.

In the zendo
notes of a bamboo flute
draw children from play.

The music echoes in the fields
touching workers who pause
before bending down again.

Having come so far
could the journey end
by this shore where comfort
tempts the odd traveller?
When across an endless sea
a different guide calls
over stiller waves.

Today they sat for the dead
for those who weep from despair
those whose tears
flow into waiting emptiness.

Another time
I could seek sun
now, content in shades
of aging oak
I study a scene
of sunburnt gulleys and hills
that rise against a lazy sky.

Here and there clouds
evoke odd images
of faces or tableaux,
perhaps forgotten dreams
or childhood schemes.

Certainly I must leave
this air of eucalyptus and sea
that cleanses the mind
and calms the senses
and go down the hill
into the web
of a dollar-fried world
to guard against
the fear or dread
of that dark insistence
that always on the left
inevitably awaits.

When trapped in cities
let the eye seek
flowers, trees or some relief
from scarred pavement.
Or follow the flight of a bird
whose cry above the traffic
can turn the self
towards larger life.